Simply Rock 70s

MW00826448

17 Rockin' Hits of the 1970s

Arranged by Dan Coates

Simply Rock 70s is a collection of some of the greatest classic rock songs from one of the most pivotal decades in pop music history. These have been carefully selected and arranged by Dan Coates for Easy Piano, making them accessible to pianists of all ages. Phrase markings, articulations, fingering and dynamics have been included to aid with interpretation, and a large print size makes the notation easy to read.

The 1970s was a time of great change in the world of music. It was an era that saw new innovations in rock, glam rock, jazz rock, progressive rock, country, reggae, funk, heavy metal, alternative pop, punk, salsa, soul and disco. Musicians thrived and became legends. The English rock group, Led Zeppelin, set a precedent for virtuosic guitar riffs, high-pitched vocals, theatrical performances, and flamboyant clothing and hairstyles. Their mega-hit, "Stairway to Heaven," has become one of the biggest-selling sheet music publications in history. Jim Croce's "Bad Bad Leroy Brown" soared to number one on the U.S. charts in the summer of 1973, selling over two million copies. The Eagles' 1976 album release of *Hotel California* won the 1977 Grammy Award for Record of the Year and is one of the best-selling albums of all time. For these reasons and more, rock music from the 1970s is exciting to explore.

After all, it is *Simply Rock 70s!*

Contents

Cat's in the Cradle

Words and Music by
Harry Chapin and Sandy Chapin
Arranged by Dan Coates

He learned to walk while I was a-way. And he was talk-in' 'fore I knew it. And
lot to do." He said, "That's o-kay." And he walked a-way, but his

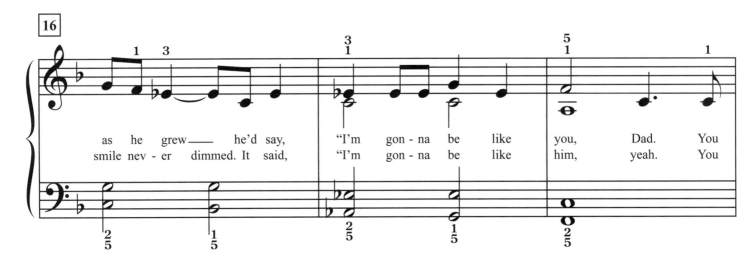

as he grew—— he'd say, "I'm gon-na be like you, Dad. You
smile nev-er dimmed. It said, "I'm gon-na be like him, yeah. You

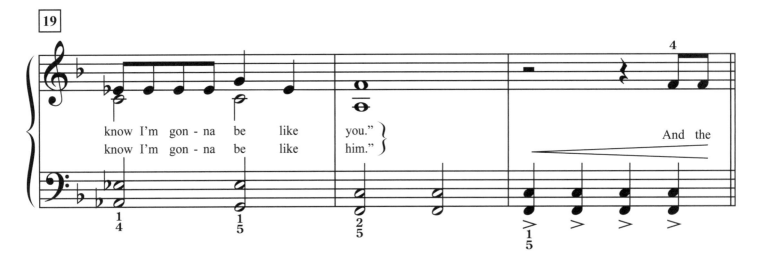

know I'm gon-na be like you." And the
know I'm gon-na be like him."

Chorus:

cat's in the cra-dle and the sil-ver spoon,— lit-tle boy blue and the man—

mf

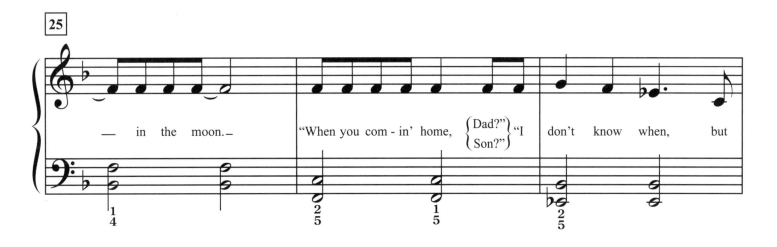

— in the moon.— "When you com-in' home, {Dad?"} {Son?"} "I don't know when, but

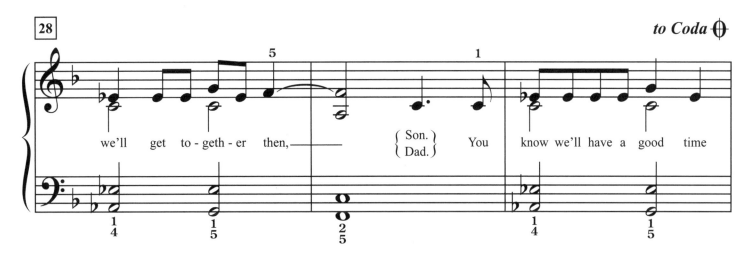

to Coda ⊕

we'll get to-geth-er then,— {Son.} {Dad.} You know we'll have a good time

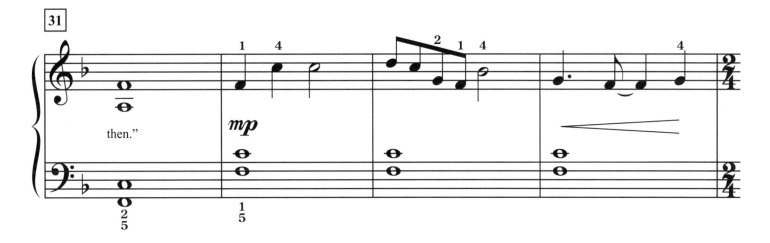

then."   *mp*

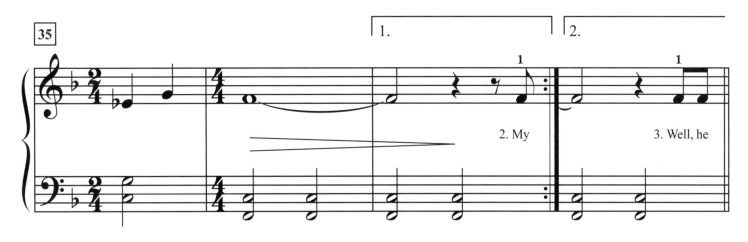

2. My   3. Well, he

came from col - lege just the oth - er day, so much like a man I just

had to say,— "Son, I'm proud of you.— Can you sit for a while?"— He

shook his head and he said with a smile,— "What I'd real - ly like, Dad, is to

D.S. al Coda

bor-row the car— keys. See you lat - er. Can I have them, please?" And the

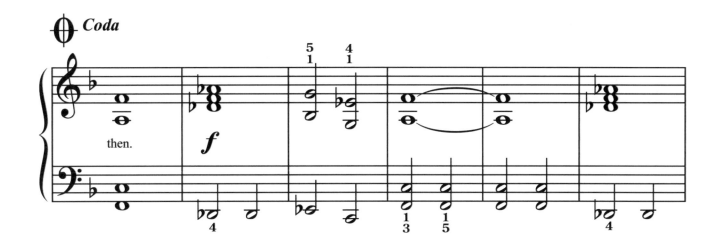

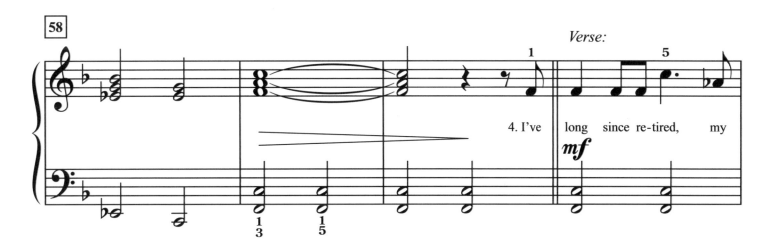

find the time.— You see my new job's a has-sle and the kids have the flu,— but it's

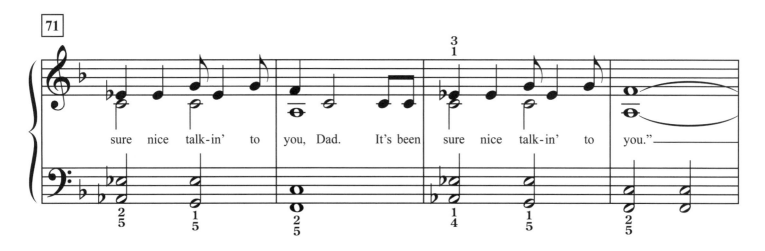

sure nice talk-in' to you, Dad. It's been sure nice talk-in' to you."——

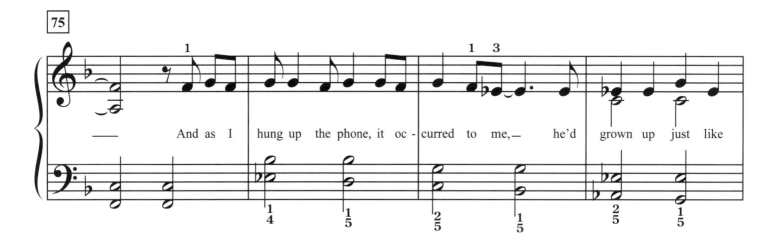

—— And as I hung up the phone, it oc-curred to me,— he'd grown up just like

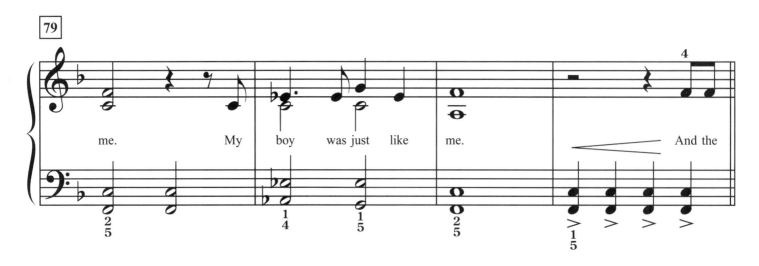

me. My boy was just like me. And the

83 *Chorus:*

cat's in the cra - dle and the   sil - ver spoon,—   lit - tle boy blue and the man—

86

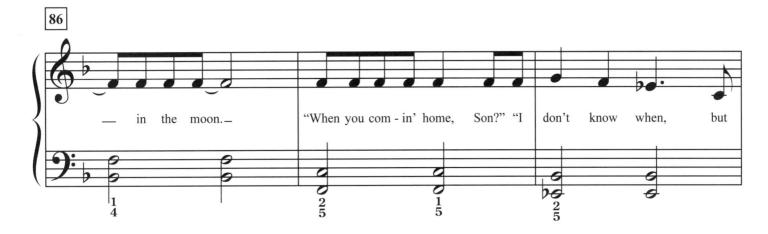

— in the moon.—   "When you com - in' home, Son?" "I don't know when, but

89

we'll get to-geth-er then,——   Dad, we're gon-na have a good time then."

93 *a tempo*

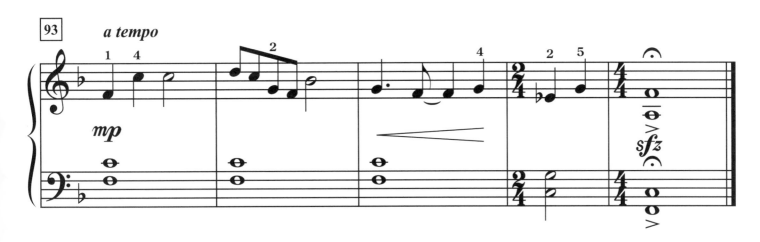

Bad Bad Leroy Brown

Words and Music by Jim Croce
Arranged by Dan Coates

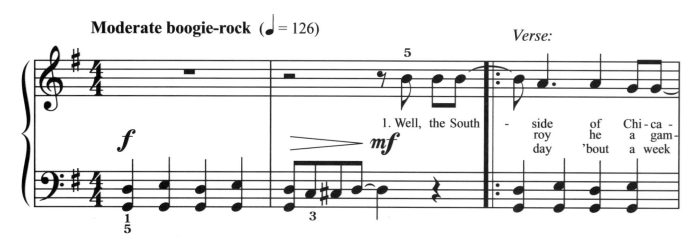

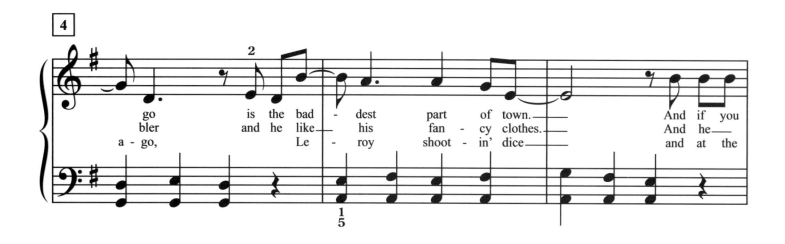

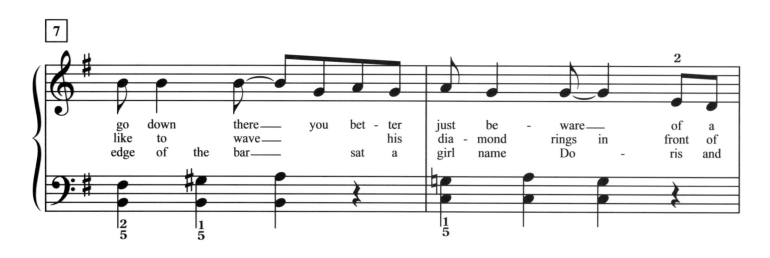

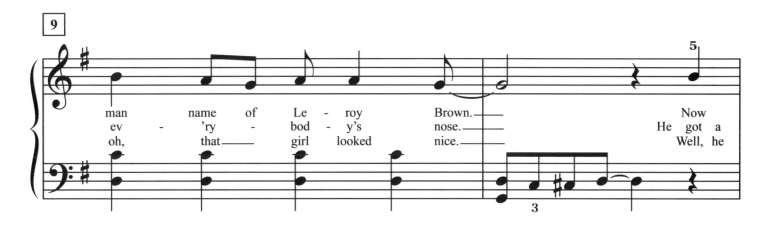

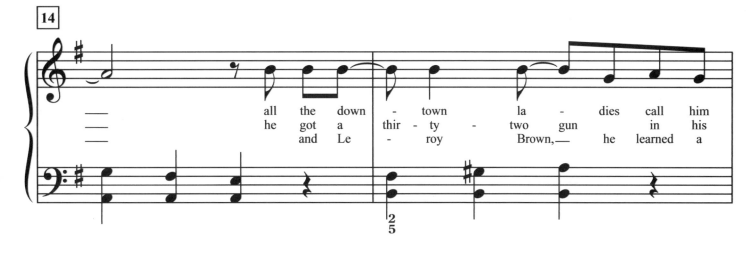

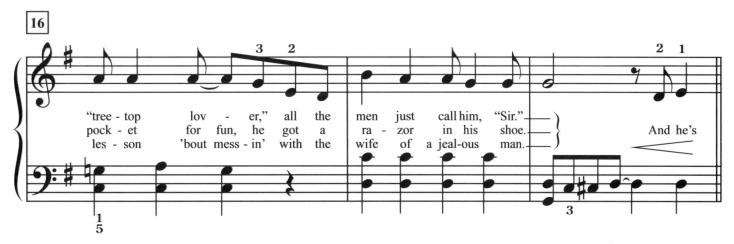

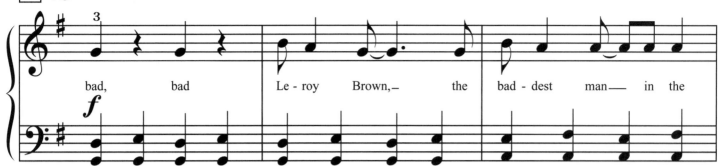

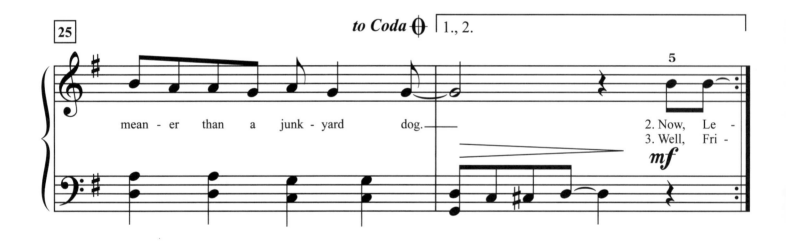

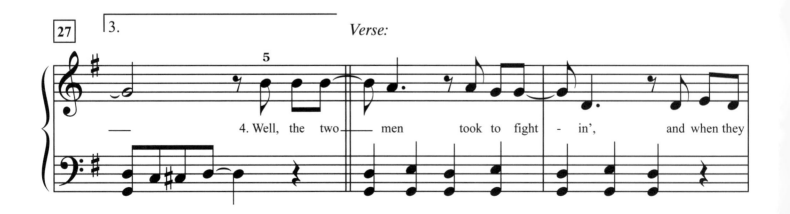

pulled them from the floor___ Le - roy looked___ like a jig -

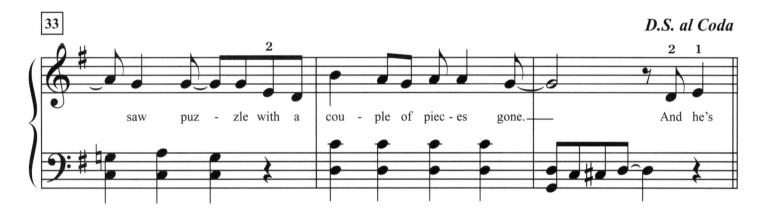

saw puz - zle with a cou - ple of piec - es gone.___ And he's

D.S. al Coda

Coda

Yes, you were bad - der than old King Kong,___

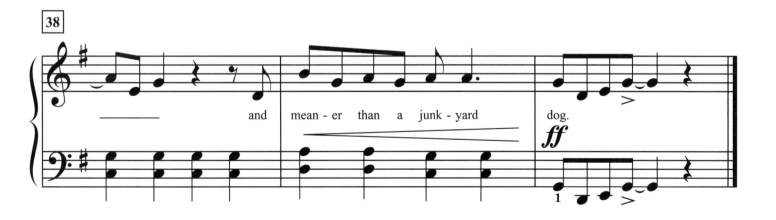

___ and mean - er than a junk - yard dog.

ff

The Best of My Love

Words and Music by
Don Henley, Glenn Frey and John David Souther
Arranged by Dan Coates

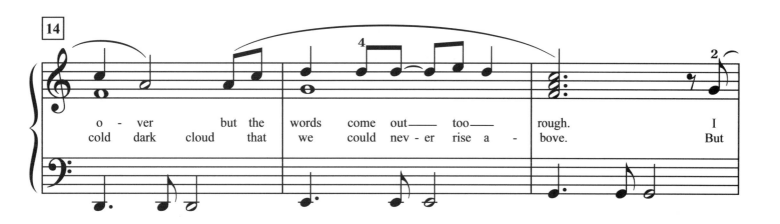

o - ver but the words come out___ too___ rough. I
cold dark cloud that we could nev - er rise a - bove. But

know you were try - in' to give me the best___ of your love.
here in my heart,___ I give you the best___ of my love.

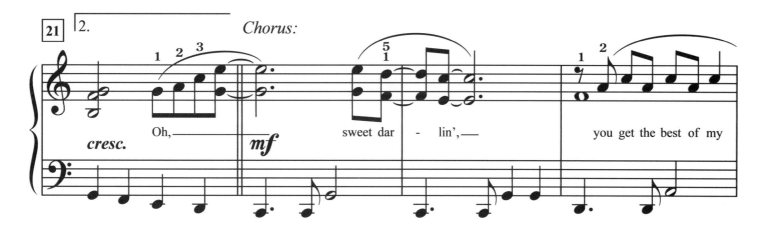

Chorus:

Oh,___ sweet dar - lin',___ you get the best of my
cresc. *mf*

love, oh,___ sweet dar - lin',___ you get the best of my

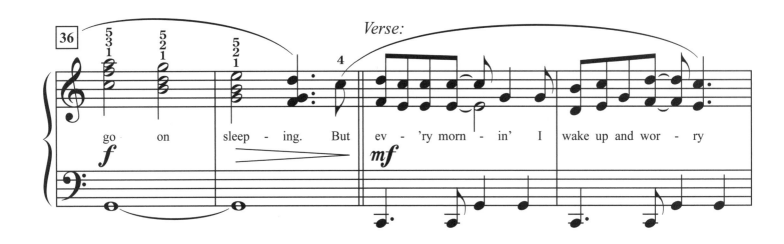

both see it slip-pin' a - way. You know we al-ways had each oth - er, ba - by,

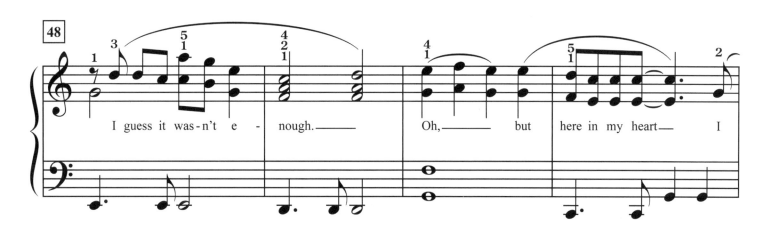

I guess it was-n't e - nough.___ Oh,___ but here in my heart___ I

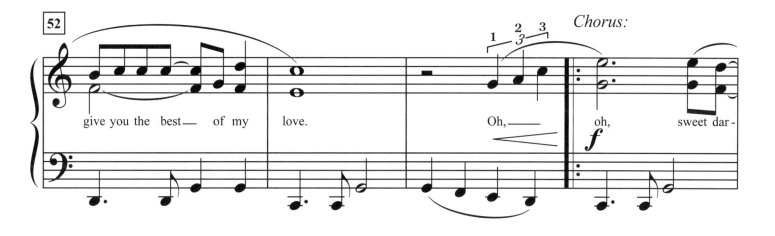

Chorus:

give you the best___ of my love. Oh,___ oh, sweet dar -

lin'___ you get the best of my love. Oh,___

Black Water

Words and Music by Patrick Simmons
Arranged by Dan Coates

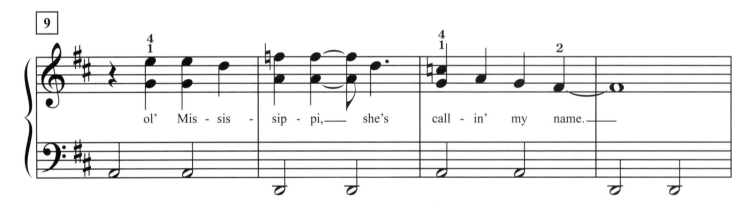

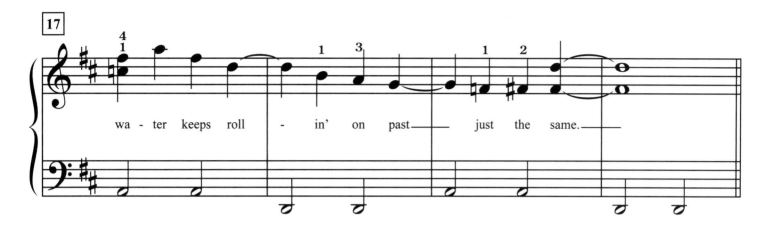

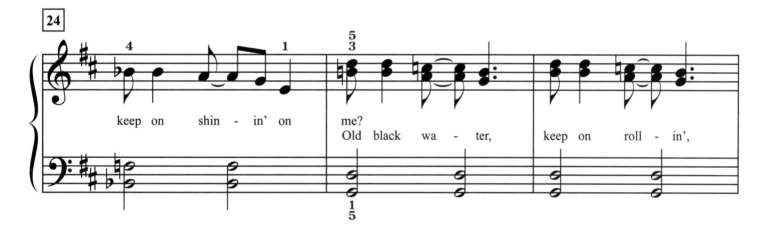

keep on roll - in, Mis - sis - sip - pi moon, won't you keep on shin - in' on

Bridge:

me? Yeah, keep on shin - in' your light, ___

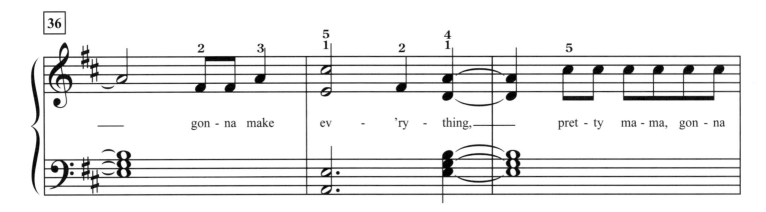

___ gon - na make ev - 'ry - thing, ___ pret - ty ma - ma, gon - na

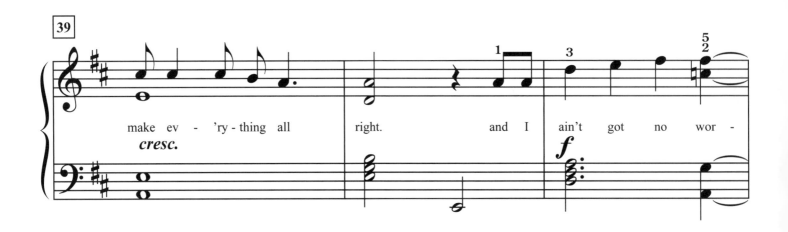

make ev - 'ry - thing all right. and I ain't got no wor -

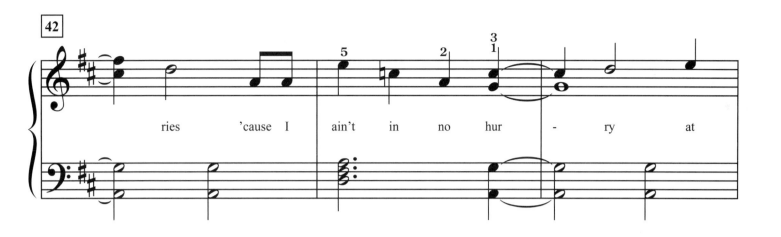

ries 'cause I ain't in no hur - ry at

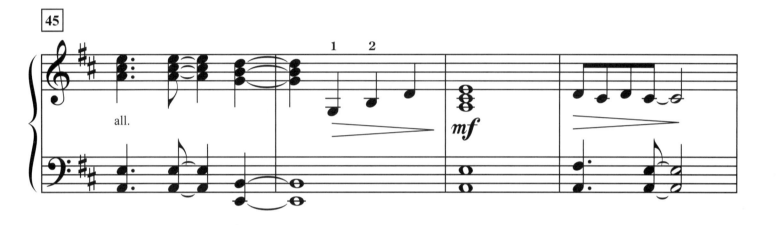

all.

Well, if it

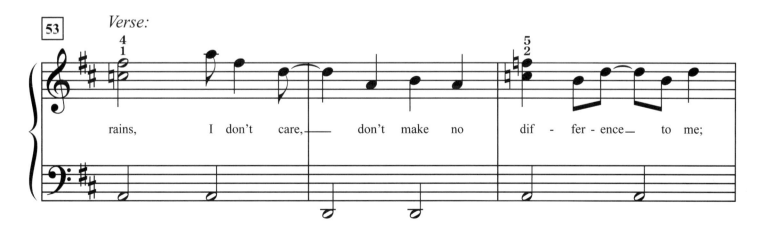

Verse:

rains, I don't care,— don't make no dif - fer - ence— to me;

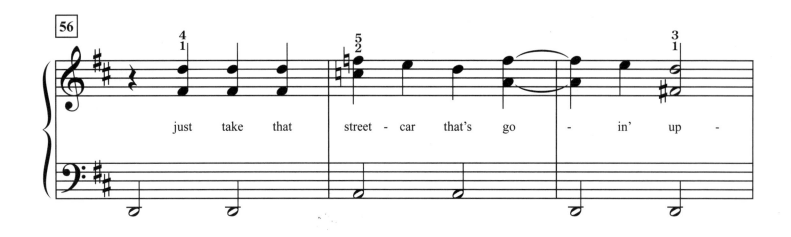

just take that street-car that's go - in' up -

town. *cresc.* Yeah, I'd like to hear some fun - ky

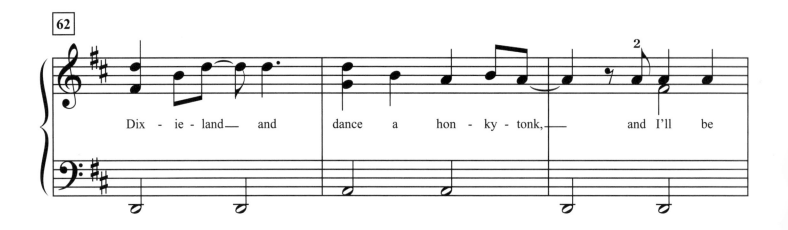

Dix - ie - land— and dance a hon - ky - tonk,— and I'll be

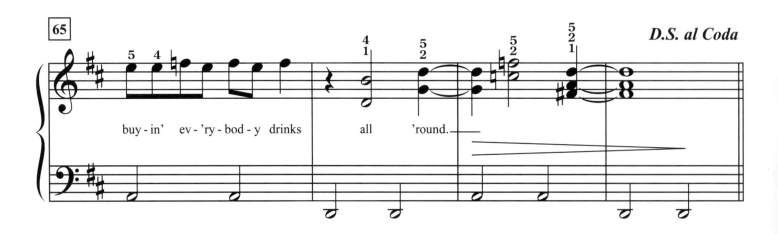

D.S. al Coda

buy - in' ev - 'ry - bod - y drinks all 'round.—

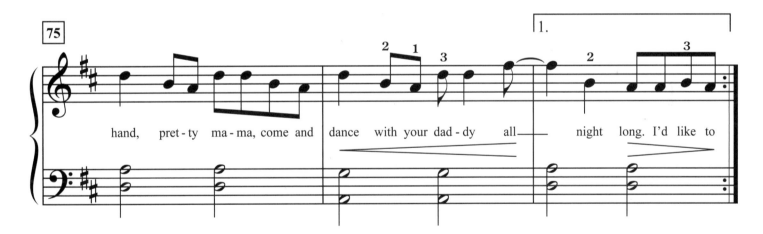

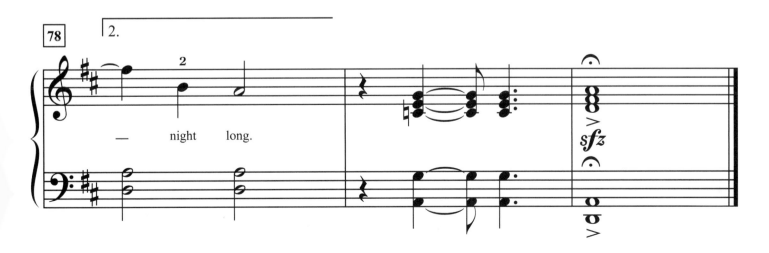

Desperado

Words and Music by
Don Henley and Glenn Frey
Arranged by Dan Coates

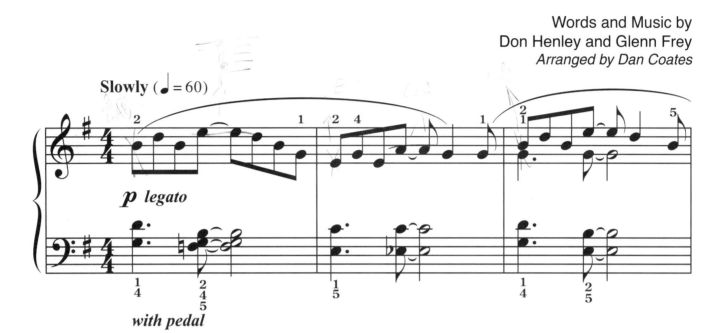

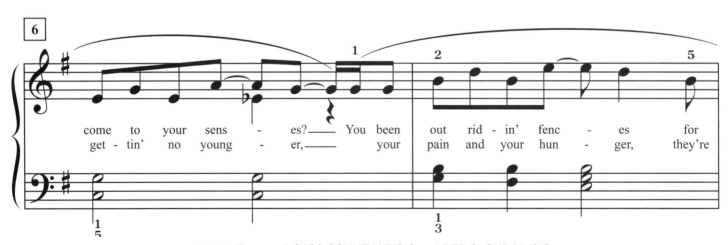

Go Your Own Way

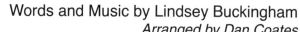

Words and Music by Lindsey Buckingham
Arranged by Dan Coates

with pedal

Verse:

1. Lov - ing you   is - n't the   right thing — to do. —   How — can I
2. Tell — me why   ev - 'ry - thing   turned a - round. —   Pack - ing up,

ev - er change   things   that — I feel?
shack - ing up   is all   you wan - na do. —

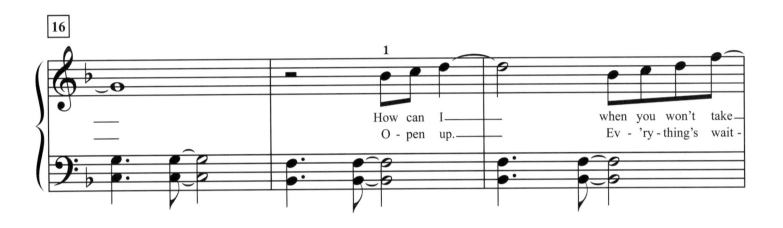

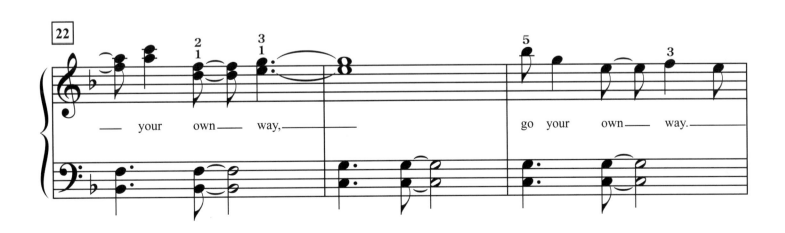

Hotel California

Words and Music by
Don Henley, Glenn Frey, and Don Felder
Arranged by Dan Coates

Layla

Words and Music by
Eric Clapton and Jim Gordon
Arranged by Dan Coates

with pedal

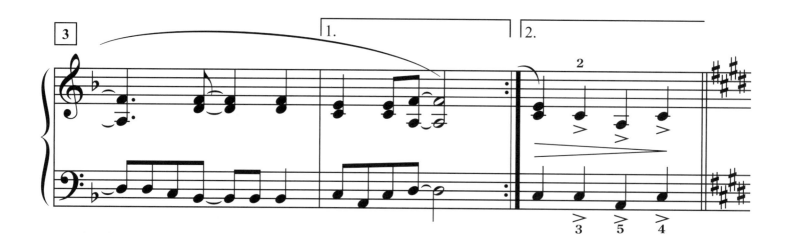

Verse:

1. What will you do when you get lone - ly?
2., 3. *See additional lyrics*

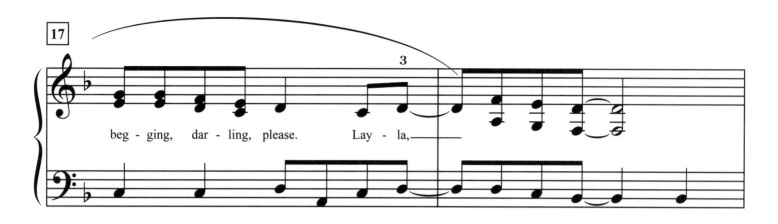

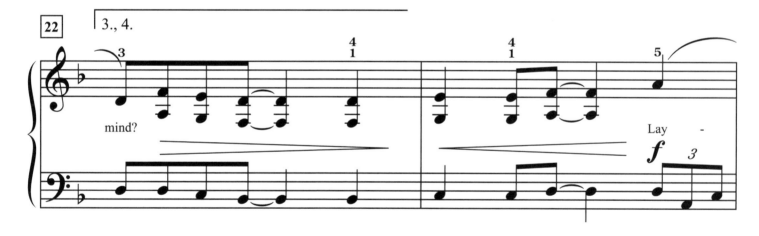

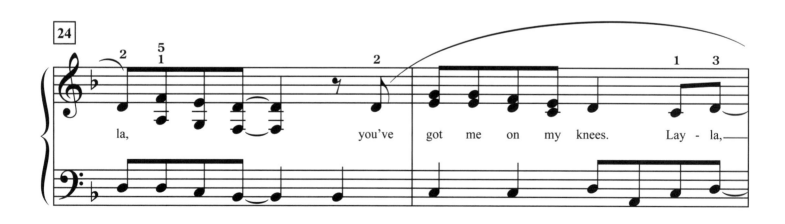

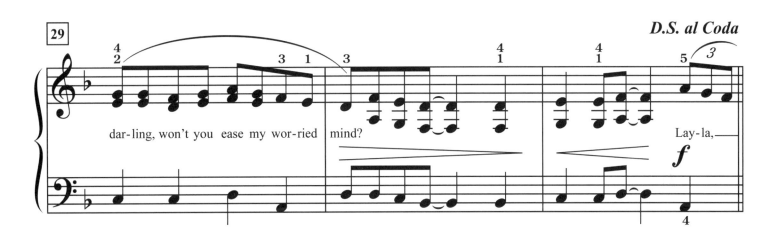

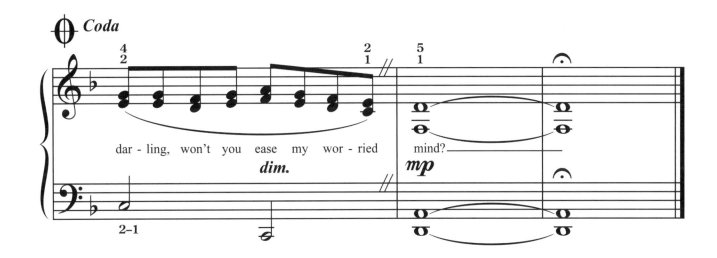

Verse 2:
Tried to give you consolation,
Your old man won't let you down.
Like a fool, I fell in love with you.
You turned my whole world upside down.
(To Chorus:)

Verse 3:
Make the best of the situation
Before I finally go insane.
Please don't say we'll never find a way
And tell me all my love's in vain.
(To Chorus:)

Old Time Rock & Roll

Words and Music by
George Jackson and Thomas E. Jones III
Arranged by Dan Coates

Bright rock beat (♩ = 128)

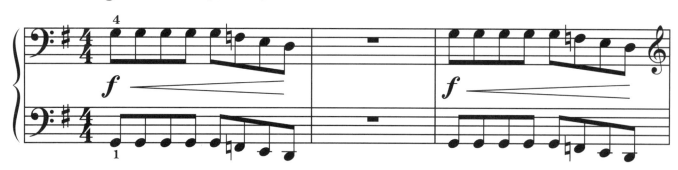

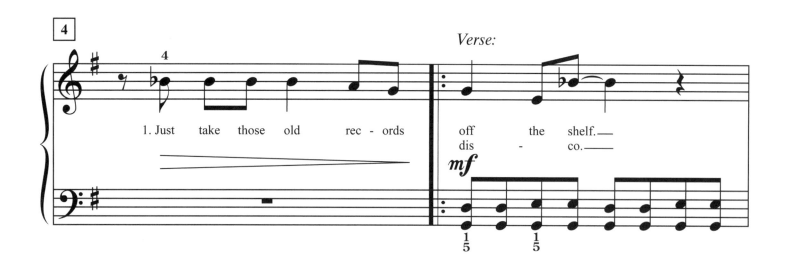

1. Just take those old rec - ords off the shelf.___
dis - co.___

I sit and lis - ten to them by my - self.___
You'll nev - er e - ven get me on the floor.___

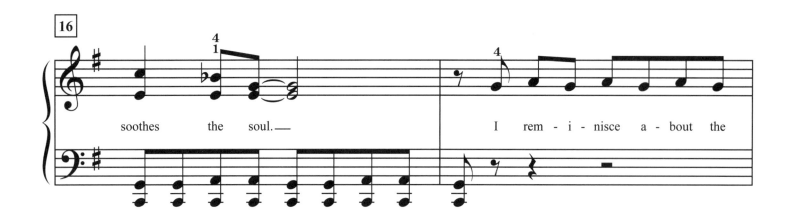

soothes the soul.— I rem - i - nisce a - bout the

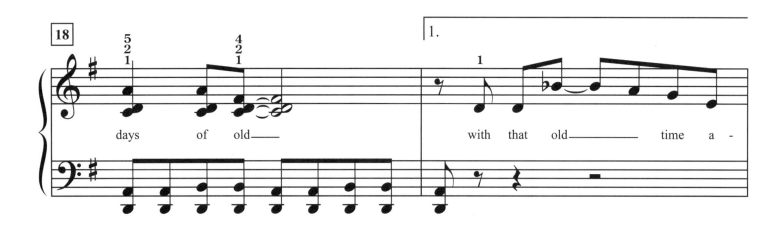

days of old— with that old——— time a -

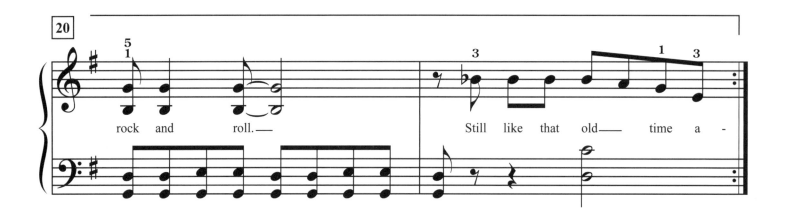

rock and roll.— Still like that old— time a -

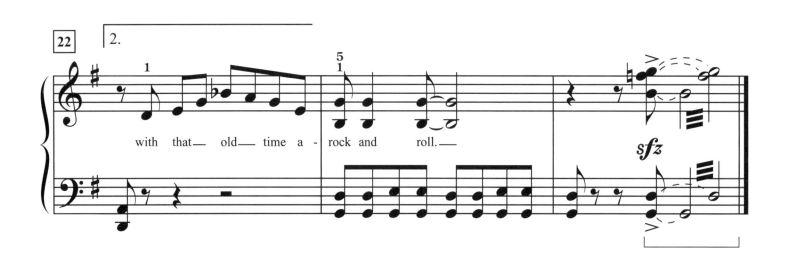

with that— old— time a - rock and roll.—

sfz

Long Train Runnin'

Words and Music by Tom Johnston
Arranged by Dan Coates

now, *cresc.*

with-out

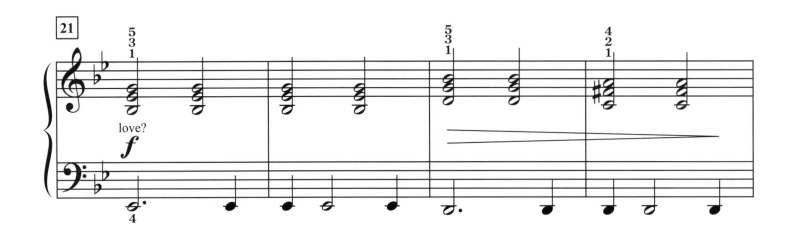

love?

f

mf

You

know I saw Miss Lu - cy down a-long— the tracks; she

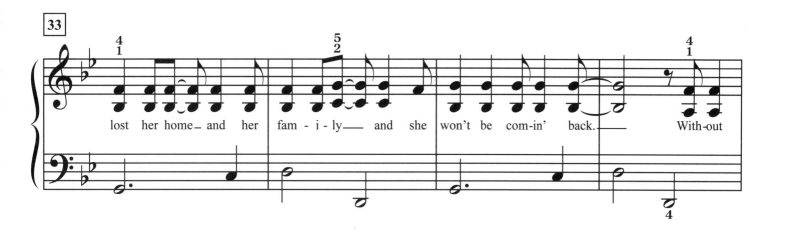

lost her home— and her fam - i - ly—— and she won't be com-in' back.—— With-out

love, where would you— be

now, cresc. with-out

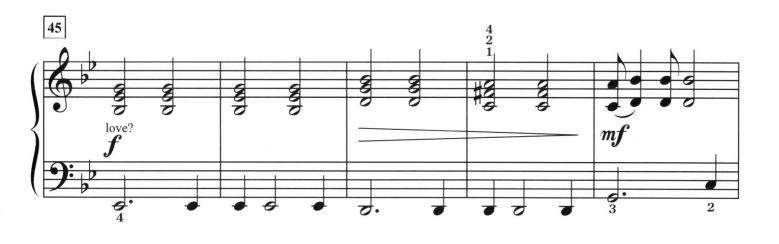

love? f mf

Well, the Il - li - no - is Cen-

tral   and the South - ern Cen - tral Freight,— got - ta keep on push - in', ma-

ma,   'cause you know they're run - nin' late.— With - out   love,

where would you— be   now,   now, now, now,

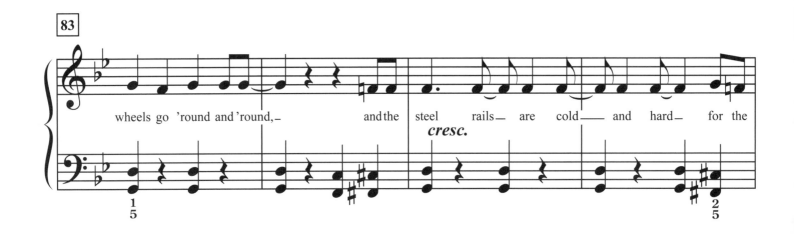

wheels go 'round and 'round,— and the steel rails— are cold— and hard— for the

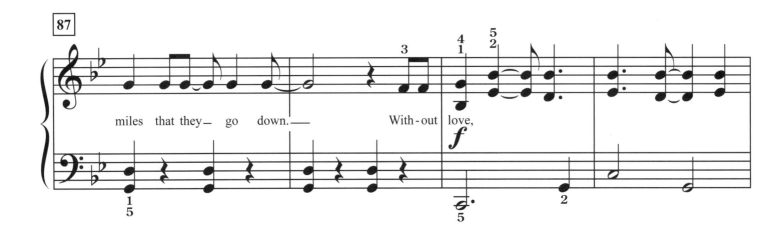

miles that they— go down.— With-out love,

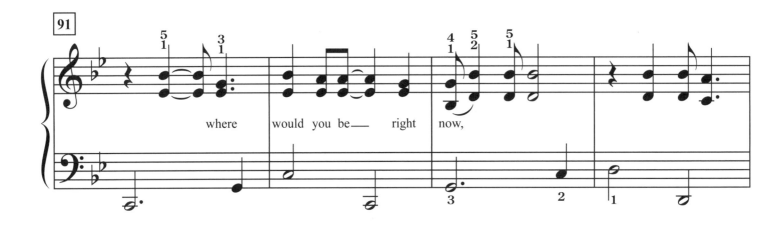

where would you be— right now,

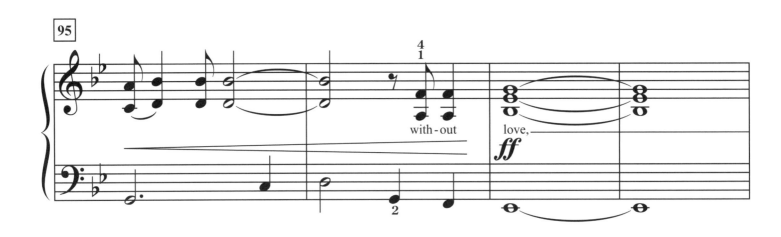

with-out love,

where would you be now?

Maggie May

Words and Music by
Rod Stewart and Martin Quittenton
Arranged by Dan Coates

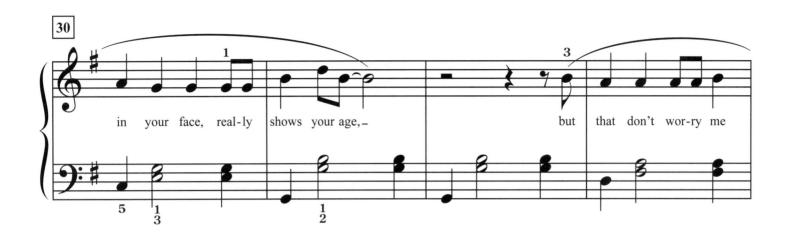

in your face, real-ly shows your age,— but that don't wor-ry me

none, in my eyes you're ev - 'ry-thing.— I laughed at all of your

jokes, my love you did-n't need to coax.— Oh, Mag-gie, I could-n't have

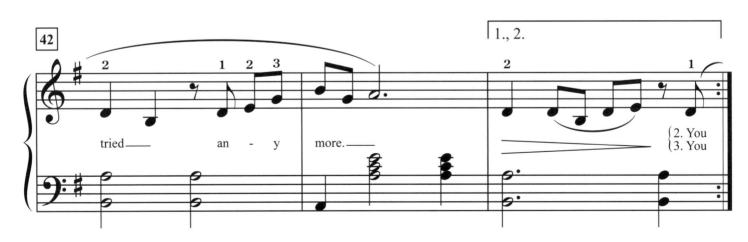

tried—— an - y more.—— 2. You / 3. You

Verse 2:

You lured me away from home, just to save you from being alone.

You stole my soul, that's a pain I can do without.

All I needed was a friend to lend a guiding hand.

But you turned into a lover, and Mother, what a lover! You wore me out.

All you did was wreck my bed, and in the morning kick me in the head.

Oh, Maggie, I couldn't have tried anymore.

Verse 3:

You lured me away from home, 'cause you didn't want to be alone.

You stole my heart, I couldn't leave you if I tried.

I suppose I could collect my books and get back to school.

Or steal my Daddy's cue and make a living out of playin' pool,

Or find myself a rock and roll band that needs a helpin' hand.

Oh, Maggie, I wish I'd never seen your face.

(To Tag:)

More Than a Feeling

Words and Music by Tom Scholz
Arranged by Dan Coates

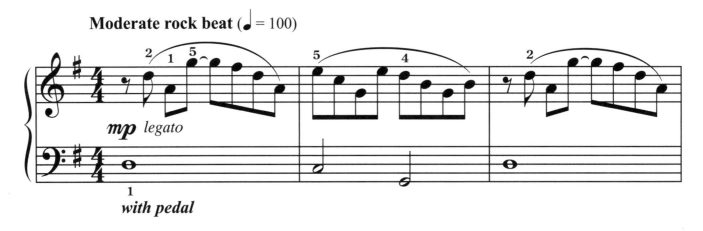

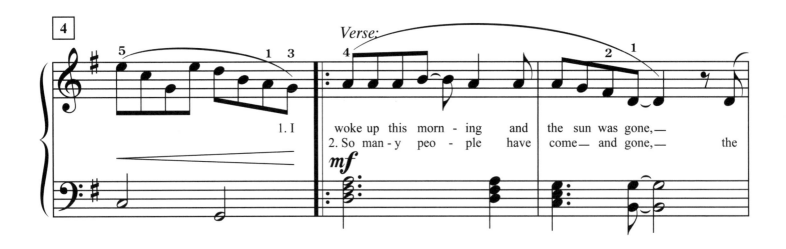

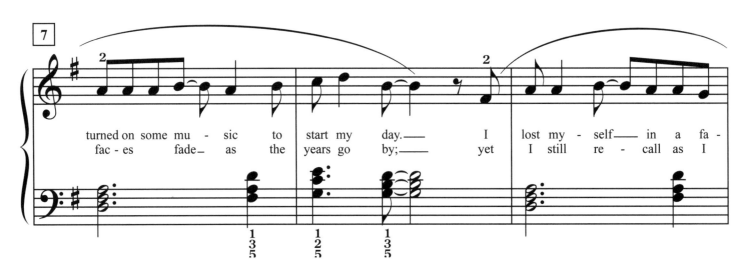

Verse 3:
When I'm tired and thinking cold,
I hide in my music, forget the day
And dream of a girl I used to know.
I closed my eyes and she slipped away.
(To Chorus:)

Peaceful Easy Feeling

Words and Music by Jack Tempchin
Arranged by Dan Coates

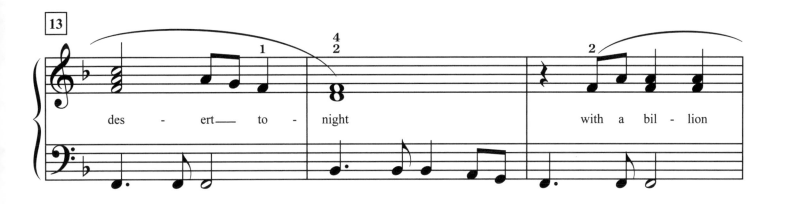

des - ert — to - night | with a bil - lion

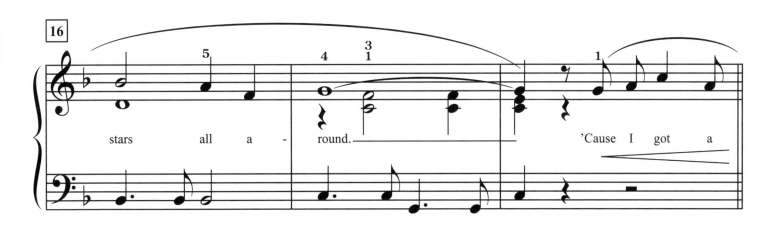

stars all a - round. _____ | 'Cause I got a

Chorus:

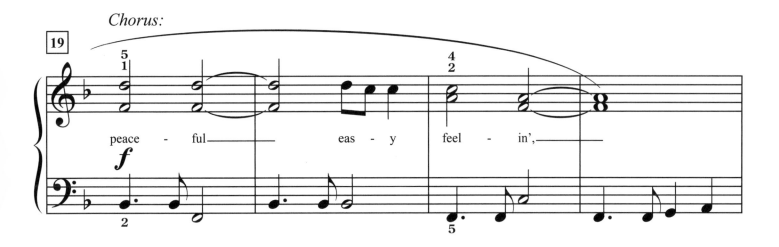

peace - ful _____ eas - y feel - in', _____

and I know you | won't let me | down, _____

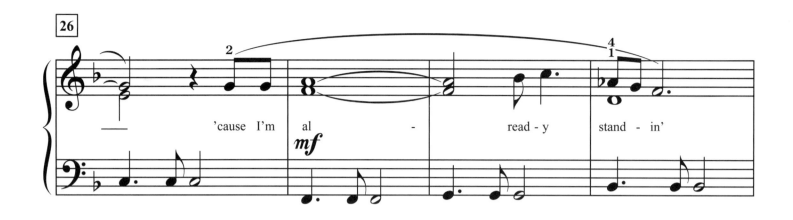

26 'cause I'm al - read - y stand - in'

mf

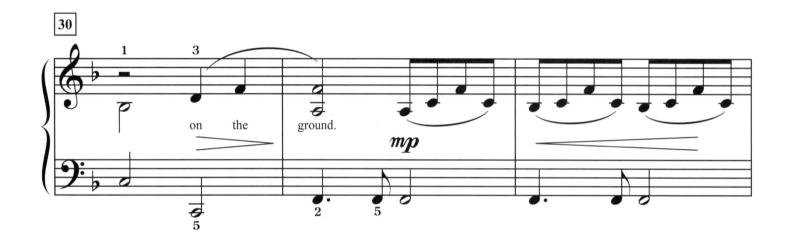

30 on the ground.

mp

33 𝄋 *Verse:*

And I found
I get
this

mf

36
out a long time——————— a - go
feel - in' I may know——————— you

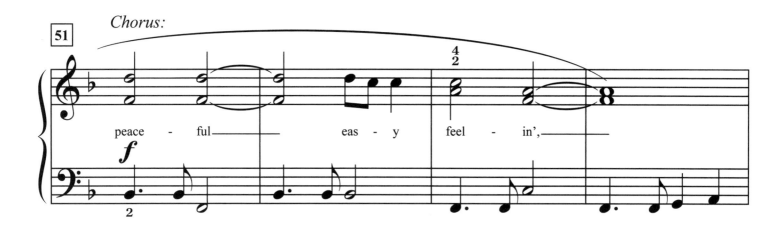

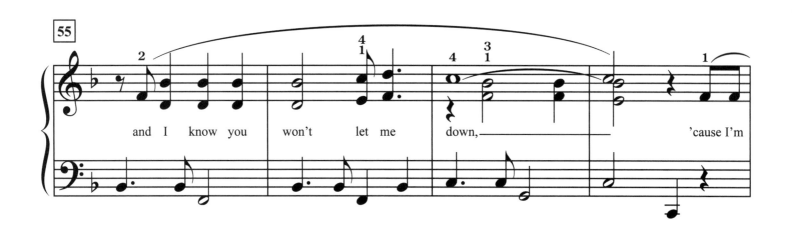

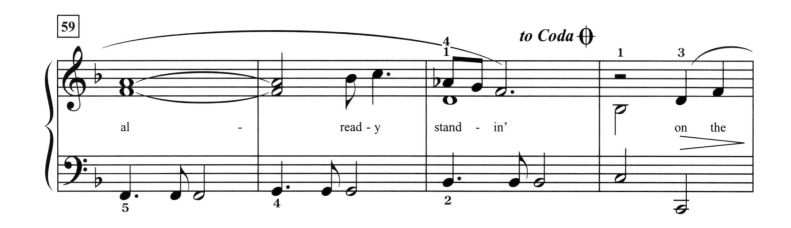

Coda

I'm—————— al - read - y

70

stand - in',   yes, I'm al - read - y

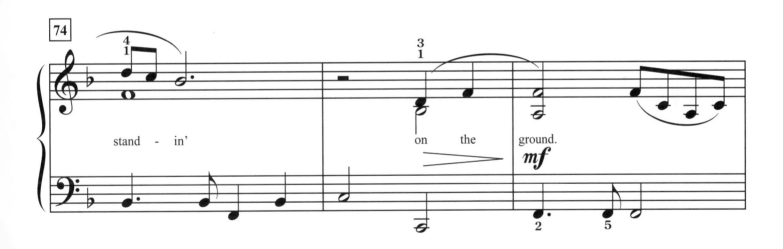

74

stand - in'   on   the   ground.   *mf*

77

rit.   *mp*

Sister Golden Hair

Words and Music by Gerry Beckley
Arranged by Dan Coates

got my - self un - dressed.___ I ain't | read - y for the al -
see it in___ my eyes?___ I been | one poor cor - re - spon -

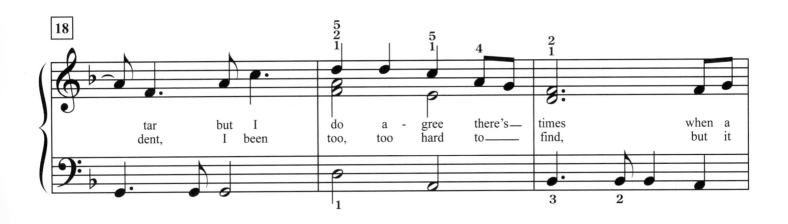

tar, but I | do a - gree there's___ times | when a
dent, I been | too, too hard to___ find, | but it

wom - an sure___ can | be a friend___ of mine.
does - n't mean___ you | ain't been on___ my mind.

1. | 2.

2. Well, I | Will you___ meet me in the mid -

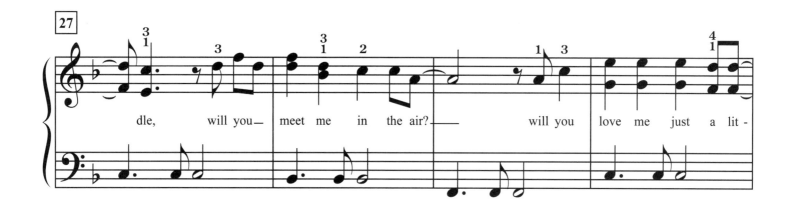

dle,   will you— meet me   in   the air?——   will you   love me   just   a lit -

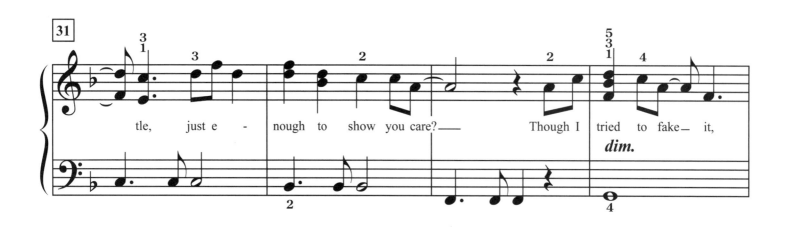

tle,   just e - nough to show you care?——   Though I tried   to fake— it,

dim.

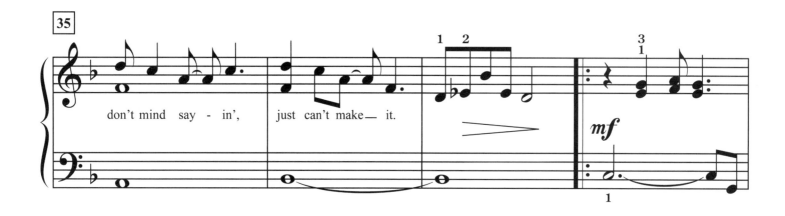

don't mind say - in',   just can't make— it.

mf

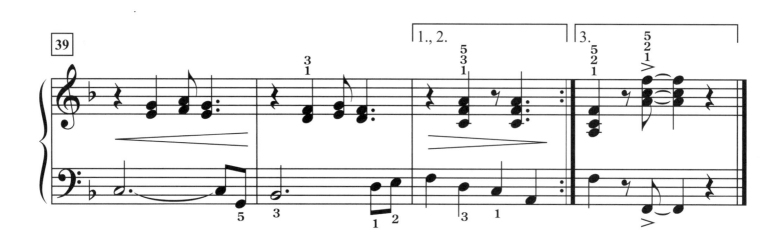

Stairway to Heaven

Words and Music by
Jimmy Page and Robert Plant
Arranged by Dan Coates

There's a la - dy who's sure all that glit - ters is gold___ and she's
sign on the wall, but she wants to be sure,___ 'cause you

buy - ing a stair - way to heav - en. When she gets there she knows if the
know some - times words have two mean - ings. In a tree by the brook, there's a

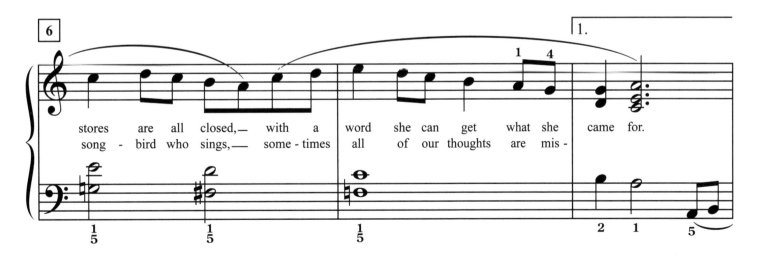

stores are all closed,___ with a word she can get what she came for.
song - bird who sings,___ some - times all of our thoughts are mis -

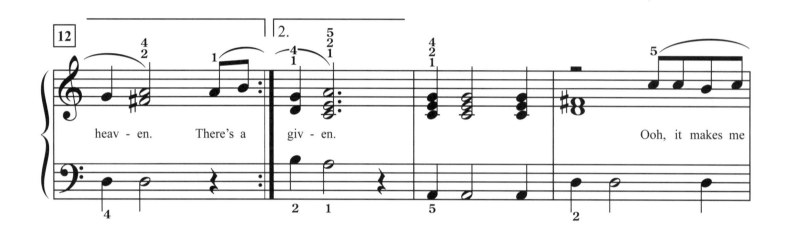

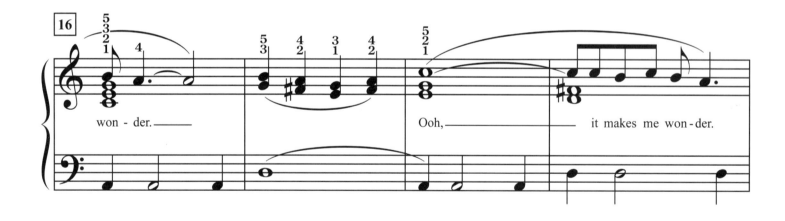

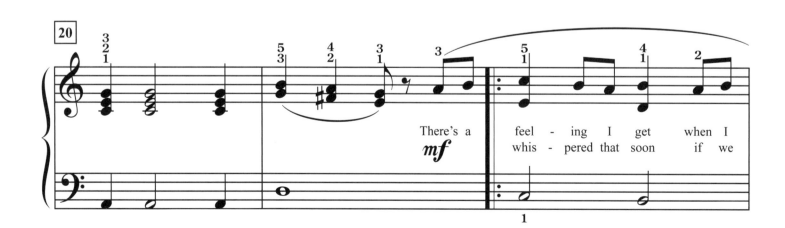

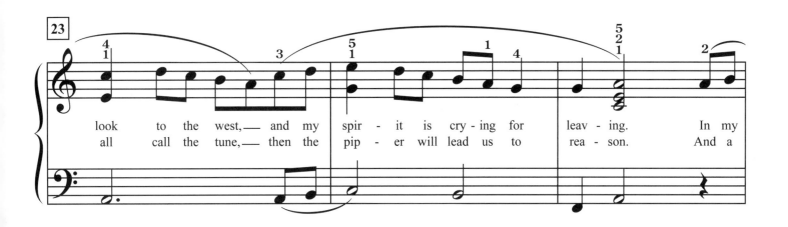

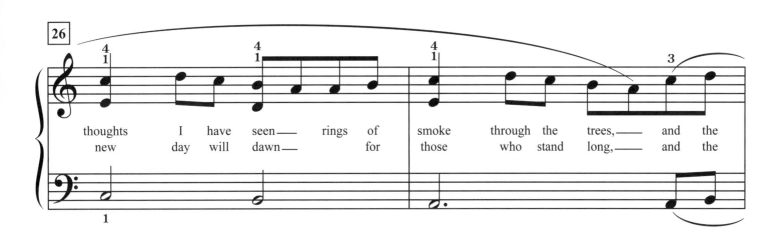

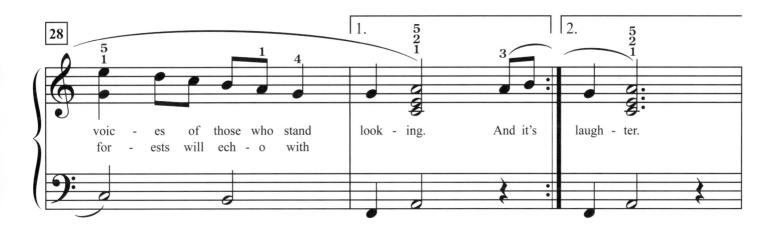

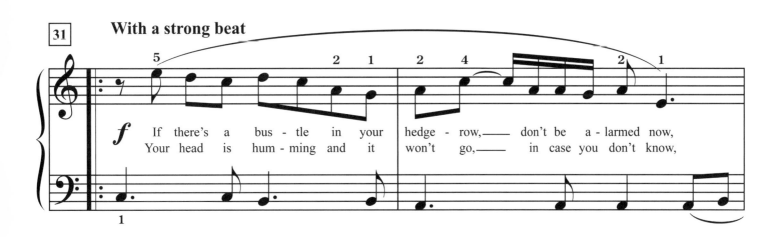

33

it's just a spring clean for the May queen.
the pip - er's call - ing you to join him.

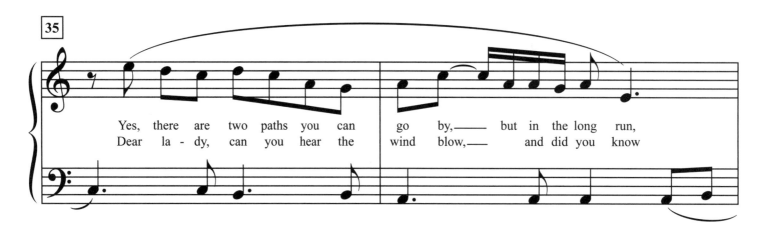

35

Yes, there are two paths you can go by,___ but in the long run,
Dear la - dy, can you hear the wind blow,___ and did you know

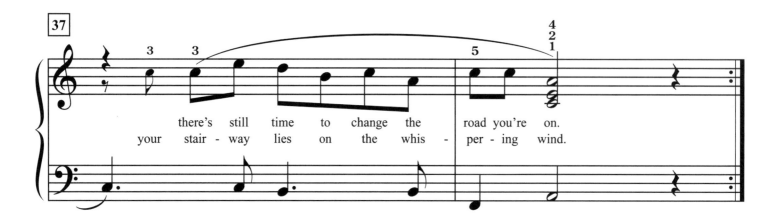

37

there's still time to change the road you're on.
your stair - way lies on the whis - per - ing wind.

39

ff

And as we wind on down the road, our shad - ows tall - er than our
how ev - 'ry - thing still turns to gold. And if you lis - ten ver - y

Time in a Bottle

Words and Music by Jim Croce
Arranged by Dan Coates

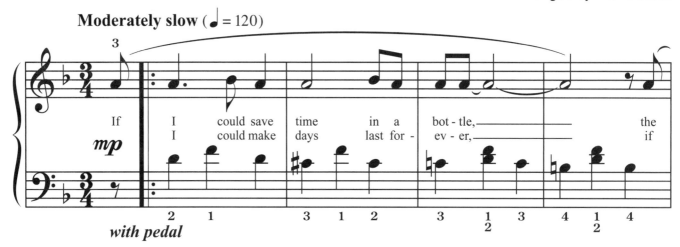

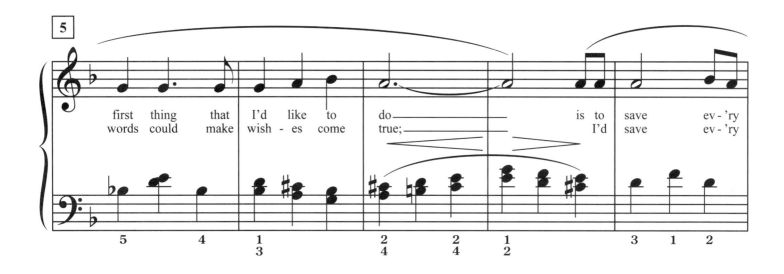

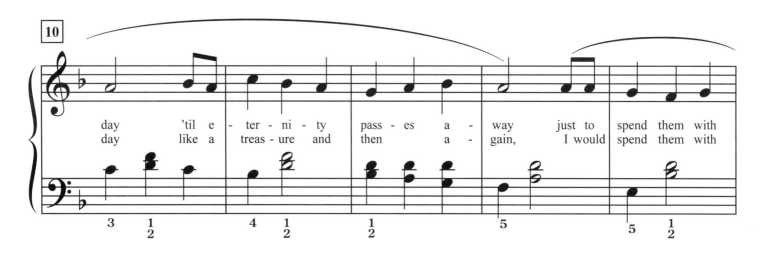

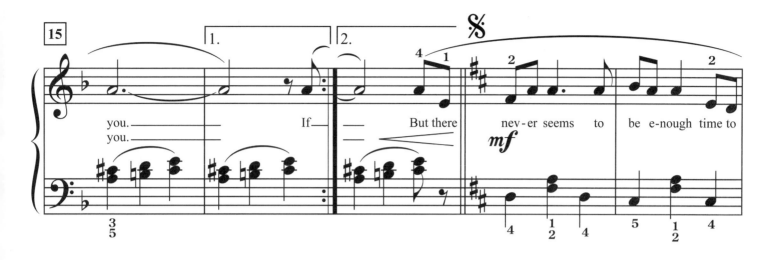

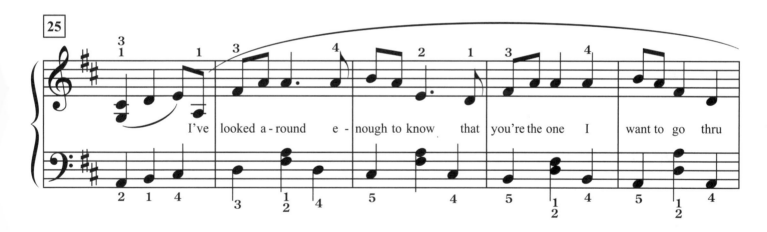

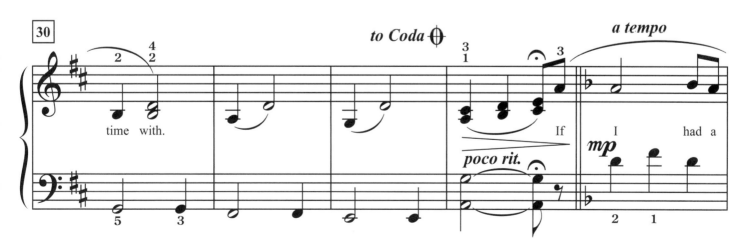

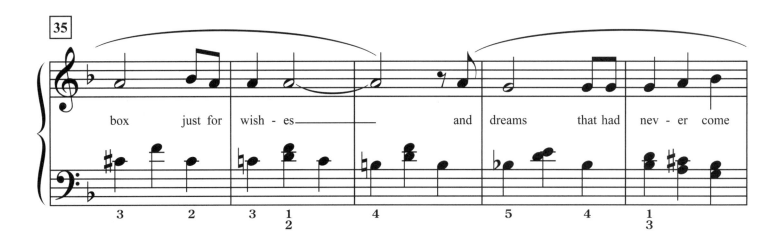

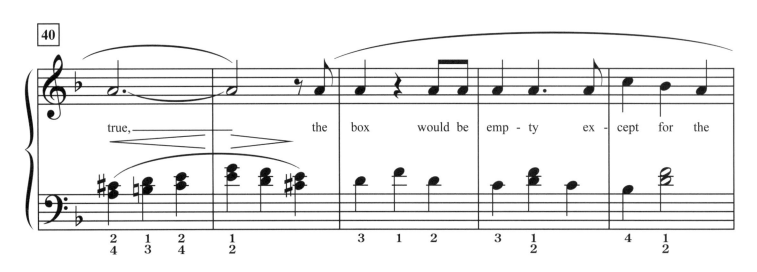

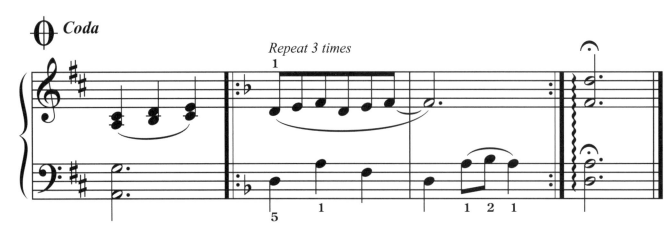

What a Fool Believes

Words and Music by
Michael McDonald and Kenny Loggins
Arranged by Dan Coates

With a bright steady tempo (♩ = 112)

for a nos - tal - gic tale, nev - er com - ing

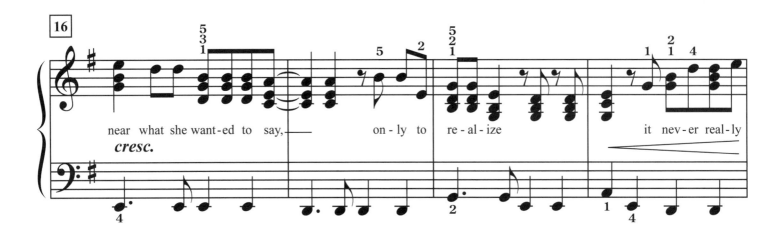

near what she want-ed to say,—— on - ly to re - al - ize it nev-er real-ly

cresc.

was. (She had a place— in his life.———

f

He nev - er made— her think twice.—————) As he

dim.

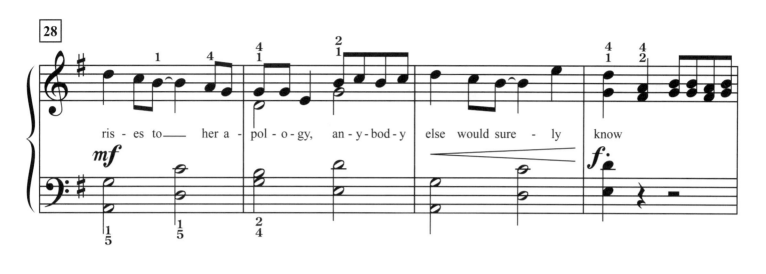

ris - es to—— her a - pol - o - gy, an - y - bod - y else would sure - ly know

he's watch - ing her go. But what a fool be -

lieves, he sees.—— No

wise man has the pow - er to rea - son a - way.

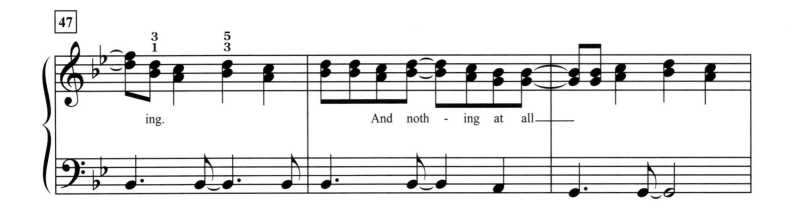

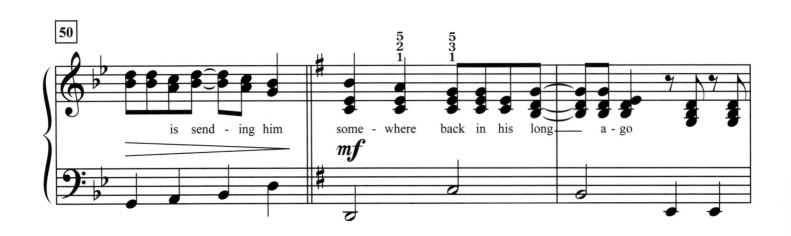

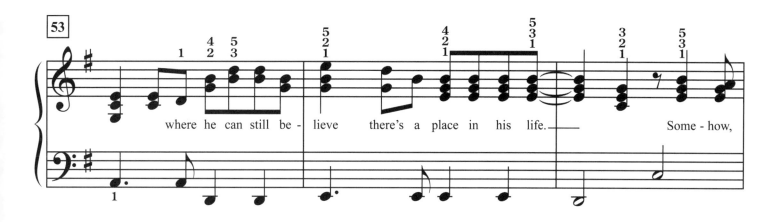

where he can still be - lieve there's a place in his life. Some - how,

some - day, *cresc.* she will re - turn!

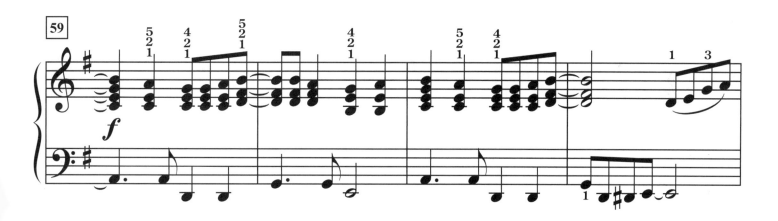

f

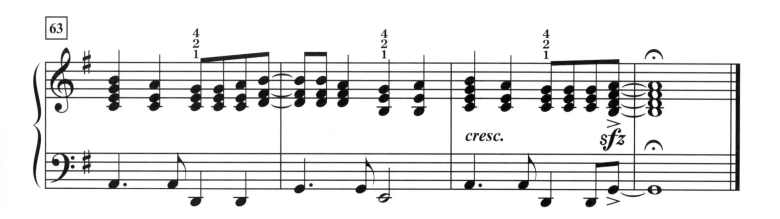

cresc. *sfz*